BEAUTY OF NATURE

BEAUTY OF NATURAL

TAMANA TAMANA

ISBN 979-888606773-6

- Acknowledgements

The most significant disease in the world today is provoking mental stress. In addition to our work, we must also enjoy the view for a few days because nature is the power that everything in this world gives us whether it is our food or our lives.

Nature has the power to remove many diseases from the body. Greenery reduces stress and provides peace of mind. So if you have a high workload most of the time and you are surrounded by psychological stress, enjoy nature to calm your mind.

A man should never hurt nature. Today's man realizes that nature has to be according to him, which is the biggest mistake. We, human beings, live in harmony with our nature and should not bring about some change in it.

Every human being on earth should enjoy this beautiful nature without disturbing the ecological balance. We need to keep it clean to prevent the destruction of the environment and nature. Nature is a lovely gift from God. Nature is gorgeous, many important forces give us happiness and healthy life.

Contents

CHAPTER ONE

- Beauty is the pleasant and appealing sensation to our eyes. It is enhanced by symmetry, color, shape, smell, scent, dynamism and vibration, brightness and darkness and other factors.

Along with all the above attributes the nature also contains breeze, water, sky, mountains, green lush meadows, trees and plants, animals, bird and flies like butterfly.

Nature's is so beautiful when the Sun rises above the horizon, so colorful and so cheering our minds to make us so energetic. ... Observing the nature for some times gives us good ideas too. The beauty of nature lies in its freshness, openness, recurrence, slow breeze touching our cheeks and the warm Sun warming our body.

Nature is the most divine creation of god around us, it is considered an integral part of mankind. Nature has bestowed us with water, air, plants and much more to make us survive on this planet. But are we paying back to our mother nature? The answer is no as we have not only failed in paying back but also exploited nature to a great extent.

Nature provides beauty all around, it's the nature that makes the surroundings attractive and worthy to live in. Human life is possible because of nature and its various boons. Mother Nature is a gift of God and must be respected just like we respect and love our mothers.

Nature is a unique blessing to us, everything created by God on this earth has some purpose and order in life. The radiant rivers, the shining valleys, huge mountains, blue oceans, white sky, the sun, the rain, the moon and the list is non-ending. All these things have some order and serve a purpose in life. Despite all this, we are still doing activities that are not only harmful but can cause real devastation to nature all around.

There are numerous creatures on this planet and every single creature serves a defined purpose in the ecosystem. Humans, on the other hand, are trying to disturb this ecosystem by entering into the places and things they are not supposed to enter. They are creating an imbalance in the ecological cycle of the environment and thus creating havoc all around.

Everything we do is dependent on nature. In fact, our life is possible because of this beautiful nature. We depend on water, air, fire for our survival and then again we are exploiting the same things we completely rely on.

We, humans, are continuously abusing our mother nature and are not even thinking about its consequences. Development is a slow process and destruction can be done in a wink of an eye.

It's the need of an hour to conserve our nature so that our generations can also enjoy and cherish in the beauties of nature. We need to create awareness among people to stop this continuous process of destruction. Human activities must be done in a sustainable way to ensure the development of a nation without causing any harm to our mother nature. It is essential to understand that we should not take advantage of some of the finest blessings of god-nature.

The beauties of nature are the greatest gifts of God to man. How unlucky are they who cannot enjoy and appreciate nature. Nature is all around us in varied aspects and shapes. We have the green charming hills, ten snow-capped mountains, and the rising and setting sun in its varied and unforgettable glory. The dew drops on the blades of grass look like iridescent pearls. The silvery moon and the twinkling stars bedeck the sky. The roaring waves in the vast ocean and the lakes which look like sheets of water add to the glorious treasure. Even the violent aspects of nature like the thundering clouds with dazzling flashes fighting, the torrential rain, and the all-powerful storm are some of the aspects of nature which Tennyson termed as nature "red in tooth and claw". But they have their own charms which captivate man and even inspire in his heart.

One can enjoy the beauties of nature in an abundant measure at a hill station. The floating clouds, the dancing springs, the winding rivulets, the all-pervading multicolor flowers, emitting sweet, soothing smell, the trees standing like sentinels with birds singing sweet harmonious songs in their branches, the cool breeze, the humming bees, the delicious fruits- all cater to human senses. Beauty lies in the eyes of the beholder on the earth, in the air, in the sky and in the ocean. His heart leaps up when he beholds a rainbow in the sky.

Nature teaches man the lesson of peace, innocence, purity, love, harmony, simplicity, hope and faith in the glory of God. Wordsworth believes that nature is the greatest store-house of wisdom, apart from being a source of eternal happiness:

Earth, a peaceful planet surrounded with water and land. A majestic planet that was once abundant with lakes, rivers, mountains, rain forest, and living creatures known as animals. The environment, ocean, and the atmosphere were free from pollution and contamination. The skies were clear and blue, lakes were clean and clear and uncontaminated. Animals roamed the land, fishes swam freely, birds chirped in the rain forest, and massive whales swam freely in the clear blue ocean. This description of Earth is the true beauty of nature and a gift from Mother Nature. Imagine the Earth free from pollution, disease, and flowing smoothly. A planet was once free from disturbance, until one creature was born and that specific creature that came to life was none other than called Neanderthals.

Nature is a way to experience life in general. A person will understand the work of art and the creation of every single living creature that is brought upon us all. Many people will destroy this beauty of nature without getting to know how nature developed over the years. They would not understand the feeling of nature itself. Many people would not get to see a footprint from an animal and get to see what kind of animal was it. They also won't understand the feeling on how fresh the environment has been for a long time. For example,

Nature is vast and full of beautiful things that comfort our physical and emotional senses. The beauty of nature is somehow immortal, infinite and eternal. The beauty of nature is a perfect reflection of the art of Allah Almighty. Natural beauty may be extinct at the moment, but as "the joy of beauty is eternal happiness", so the effect of that beauty on the mind can never be in vain.

Natural beauty is a treasure that will never end. Nature has many faces. They are everywhere. The human eye is always in contact with good things.

One of the many beautiful features of nature is the sunrise and sunset. A person with a sense of beauty will never be able to ignore the beauty of the red light of the rising sun and the fading glow of the stars. Likewise, the beauty of sunset has inspired many sensitive and artistic people to compose verses of praise, write beautiful prose and paint, and capture the event with a cloth or a camera forever.

Another aspect of natural beauty can be found in the night sky. Arriving at your destination, the glowing stars and the glowing moon of the moon have nothing in common. Under the influence of the moonlight, this world also becomes a beautiful world and a dream world.

The changing seasons have their beauty that has fascinated the human mind for centuries and will continue to impress until the end of the universe. Spring is the most beautiful of the seasons and is undoubtedly the queen of the seasons. During this period, the earth was filled with lush vegetation, colors, and aromas. Spring is a time of beauty and love, hope and happiness, life and happiness. Forests, lush plains, fields, and meadows prowl the lush vegetation to attract attention. Spring has endless and countless charms and beauty. Autumn has its golden, brown and mature colors. A life that started in the spring matures in the fall. This is a time for maturity and maturity. Summer is a season that helps the ripening process. It has its charms and beauty in the form of the most delicious fruits and vegetables.

Cold winters, snow and fog have other advantages. It is

a season of white, grey and black. Snow and ice have a fantastic effect on the human mind and are not as appealing as the dark clouds and the wind.

On the other hand, nature has the beauty of the refreshing sky, the snowcapped mountains, and the deep green valleys. On the other hand, it has the mysteries and incomparable beauty of the deep blue sea. Nature preserves the beauty of the desolate desert and empty sand during the oasis. Its long date trees that grow in the spring of freshwater show excellent scenes for tired and thirsty travelers.

Nature has endless treasures of beauty in the form of various beautiful living creatures. The world of birds, beasts, reptiles, and fish is teeming with life and millions of species of all kinds, in size and color and on the earth, in the sky and the water. They are everywhere and at all times. They adorn the environment by simply being present.

Humans, the "crown of creation," is by no means the most beautiful. Beauty lies in the condition of the body, the brain and the soul. It exists like human nature, such as mother, sister, brother and father, friend and companion.

Beauty is present in the child's smiling face, the mother's prayerful hand and the anxious state of the father. Beauty is like the reassuring handshake of a friend, the gentle touch of a brother and the love of a caring sister.

Undoubtedly beauty exists in man, in the environment, green fields, high mountains and small hills, in the moonlight and stars. Nature is full of the beauty that exists, almost everything scattered about us. "Beauty, truth, truth, and Beauty," as the saying goes.

How to Protect Nature?

We can protect nature by taking care of a few key things like-

- By planting more and more trees. Soil erosion can be prevented by planting trees.
- By preventing soil erosion, we can protect nature's beautiful oceans, rivers, and the ozone layer.
- Sources Prevent excessive use of natural resources. There is a need to use wisely without wasting available resources.
- Hunting for wild animals should be stopped for wildlife protection.
- Farmers should be taught for mixed cropping systems, fertilizers, pesticides, pesticides, and crop rotation. There is a need to promote the use of fertilizers and organic fertilizers
- Deforestation should be regulated.
- Eating a Rainwater Harvesting System should be installed.
- The use of renewable resources, such as solar, water, and wind energy, should be promoted.
- Water used in agricultural processes must be recycled.
- Car-pooling is the best way to diminish fossil fuel consumption.
- As per limit to use of paper and promote recycling.
- Save energy by using fluorescent bulbs instead of old light bulbs. Also, turn off light and electronic items when not needed.
- We must try our best to keep the nature around us clean.
- All measures should be taken to prevent all types of environmental pollution.
- We must never distort the balance of nature for our own sake because it will eventually become the most

significant cause of human destruction.

- **Importance of Nature**

Our nature has given us a wide variety of flowers, birds, animals, trees, blue skies, lands, rivers, oceans, and mountains. God created all these things to improve man's life, so we must never harm this natural wealth.

Nature has given much to man, but man is always busy destroying it. Humans have created many natural-destructive causes for their benefit, such as environmental pollution, global warming, and the greenhouse effect.

There are so many innovations in the world of technology today, but nobody cares how these innovations affect nature. Therefore, before doing anything, we must assume that doing so would benefit or harm nature.

We need to keep our environment as clean as possible, not spread pollution and promote deforestation in our area. Millions of houses are being built every day, for which millions of trees are being cut down; we need to plant new plants every day so that the trees in nature are balanced.

Just as important as man is in nature, animals are just as important. Life on earth is impossible without animals. Therefore, to protect our environment, the protection of the organism is also critical.

Many countries of the world have built wild sanctuaries to protect animals. Besides, in every country, there are government agencies for the protection of organisms that live there.

10 Lines on Nature

- Wordsworth, a loyal nature lover, believes that nature is a storehouse of joy and happiness.

- It is the eternal source of divine beauty.
- It is healing to a friend, guide, and stewardship and person. A sick body or a broken mind feels very relaxed, courageous, and relaxed in the lap of nature.
- It gives new energy and emotion to a person in the form of God.
- The immense beauty of nature is full of blessings for humanity.
- Flowing rivers, flowing noise, flowing winds, raging waterfalls, mighty flowers, and high mountains add to the natural beauty of the moon.
- Nature fills our lives with genuine happiness, goodness, and happiness.
- For the lover of nature, every object of the earth is alive as a person.
- Great nature lover Wordsworth wrote: "Nature is a soul."
- We must respect the gift of nature and use nature according to the rules.
- **The Bottom Line**

  There are some major transformational forces in nature that control our mood and behavior. Nature is essential to a healthy life. Therefore, we must keep it clean and safe for future generations. We cut down trees and forests. We have to keep it intact. We must not pollute the oceans and rivers to save the ozone layer safe. And all our lives are undisturbed.

  Nature is an important and integral part of mankind. It is one of the greatest blessings for human life; however, nowadays humans fail to recognize it as one. Nature has been an inspiration for numerous poets, writers, artists and more of yesteryears. This remarkable creation inspired them to write poems and stories in the glory of it. They truly valued nature which reflects in their works even today. Essentially, nature is everything we are surrounded by like the water we drink, the air we breathe, the sun we soak in, the birds we hear chirping, the moon we gaze at and more. Above all, it is rich and vibrant and consists of both living and non-living things. Therefore, people of the modern age should also learn something from people of yesteryear and start valuing nature before it gets too late.

Significance of Nature

Nature has been in existence long before humans and ever since it has taken care of mankind and nourished it forever. In other words, it offers us a protective layer which guards us against all kinds of damages and harms. Survival of mankind without nature is impossible and humans need to understand that.

If nature has the ability to protect us, it is also powerful enough to destroy the entire mankind. Every form of nature, for instance, the plants, animals, rivers, mountains, moon, and more holds equal significance for us. Absence of one element is enough to cause a catastrophe in the functioning of human life.

We fulfill our healthy lifestyle by eating and drinking healthy, which nature gives us. Similarly, it provides us with water and food that enables us to do so. Rainfall and sunshine, the two most important elements to survive are derived from nature itself.

Further, the air we breathe and the wood we use for various purposes are a gift of nature only. But, with technological advancements, people are not paying attention to nature. The need to conserve and balance the natural assets is rising day by day which requires immediate attention.

In order to conserve nature, we must take drastic steps right away to prevent any further damage. The most important step is to prevent deforestation at all levels. Cutting down of trees has serious consequences in different spheres. It can cause soil erosion easily and also bring a decline in rainfall on a major level.

Polluting ocean water must be strictly prohibited by all industries straightaway as it causes a lot of water shortage. The excessive use of automobiles, AC's and ovens emit a lot of Chlorofluorocarbons' which depletes the ozone layer. This, in turn, causes global warming which causes thermal expansion and melting of glaciers.

Therefore, we should avoid personal use of the vehicle when we can, switch to public transport and carpooling. We must invest in solar energy giving a chance for the natural resources to replenish.

In conclusion, nature has a powerful transformative power which is responsible for the functioning of life on earth. It is essential for mankind to flourish so it is our duty to conserve it for our future generations. We must stop the selfish activities and try our best to preserve the natural resources so life can forever be nourished on earth.

Nature, in which everything is present. Every planet, satellite, star, air, water, creature, human being, life, etc. in the universe is natural. Human beings have been progressing day by day, he can never win over it.

God created a very beautiful nature. Everyone on our planet, except man, is living acc to the law of nature. We can see the beauty of God in nature.

We must respect God's creation. Humans must take steps to **nature conservation** also.

Nature is so beautiful that everyone can feel the particles present in it. Rivers, streams, animals, oceans, mountains, greenery, etc. have their own significance in this.

When it rains, every creature blooms. Greenery appears all around & everyone can enjoy **the beauty of nature anytime.**

There is a novelty in birds and animals. In everything comes the essence. It provides us with all kinds of facilities. Oxygen is obtained through the air. There is no need to be idle to enjoy the sights of nature.

Nature is always beautiful which captivates every heart. It can be seen on our planet all the time.

When the birds start chirping before sunrise in the morning. The sound of their chirping sounds like a piece of beautiful music.

Importance of Nature and Environment in our life in points

The rooster has a natural tendency to crow in the morning. It acts as a natural alarm. When the sun is rising in the morning, its redness and rays offer a beautiful view.

This scene gives us a sense of humor. When we see birds flying in the sky, the mind feels very happy.

The view of the rising sun is very beautiful in the mountains. When its light falls on snow or glaciers in the mountains, its brightness is noticeable.

Seeing sun rays falling on the mountains, it seems that the mountains are also speaking and thanking the sun. When you look at naturally formed mountains, it seems as if their shape resembles a shape.

Life is a little harder for people living close to nature in the mountains but they are healthier and enjoy the **natural beauty of nature** than people living in the plains. Clouds and deep ravines in the mountains create wonderful scenery.

Some of the natural mountain scenery cannot be described in words. When it rains in the mountains, the mind is refreshed. The raindrops create excitement in the mind.

The natural waterfalls increase the beauty of nature, everyone wants to take a bath under that waterfall. Usually, when tourists go for a walk, they take bathe under these waterfalls. It is fun to see the natural scenery of the rivers & **the beauty of nature quotes.**

The water flowing in the form of waterfalls in the mountains changes its shape when it reaches the plains. This water is converted from waterfalls to rivers..

Everyone knows and seen that the rivers look very beautiful from a distance. The birds sitting in them look very attractive.

When it comes to **enjoying the beauty of nature**, the desert offers a completely different view. The enchanting sand dunes and high and low sand dunes spread all over the desert captivate the mind.

The waves on the sand seem very attractive as the wind blows. When vehicles move in the desert, the sand blows here and there with the wind.

Seeing the beauty of nature, it seems as if snakes made of sand are crawling on the road. The desert is hot in day time but cold at night.

The naturally collected water in the desert dunes looks like a gold-framed inlaid circle. The sun's rays falling in it look like pearls shining.

The sky appears blue and the white clouds floating in the air take on different shapes in the daytime. That too becomes a captivating sight &

Importance and the beauty of nature in Islands & oceans

Forests also exist in nature. **Exploring the beauty of nature** in forests, many views can be seen. Many people go to see the animals in the forest.

They also take photos of them. As it can be seen hunting lions, elephants, deer, etc. There are many birds and animals in the forests that cannot be seen in ordinary life.

People who live in hot areas also like the snow scattered in snowy areas. In some places of the world, the sun does not rise for long and in some places, the sun sets for only two to four hours.

You can see the **natural beauty** of such an area in those places. The beauty of nature is especially appealing to the islands.

Surprisingly, the islands in the middle of the ocean are stable and when viewed from the sky, they look like spots in the ocean. There are volcanoes in many places & **the beauty of nature quotes.**

Boiling lava can be seen in them. When a volcano erupts, its lava comes out with a lot of pressure. The lava scene looks like a fountain.

As stated earlier, everything in nature has its own significance. We see many trees and plants.

Some trees are so large and widespread that it is difficult to find the root. Look at them, it looks like a palace of trees.

Flowering plants also enhance the beauty of nature. The smiling faces of the flowers always give positivity. Many flowers are carnivorous.

In summer & winter, **nature and its beauty** come in different forms. When autumn comes, the leaves of many trees fall off on their own.

Before the fall, the leaves of many trees change color, enhancing the natural beauty of nature. Then during the spring, the trees have new leaves and flowers.

They also look great and beautiful. The winter fog freezes the fog all around but it seems that there is a blanket of snow everywhere. The drops on the trees and plants look like pearls.

In many places, it always rains. As the highest rainfall in the world occurs in Chirapunji.

See the beauty of nature after rain and when the sun's rays fall on the particles floating in the air, forming a rainbow. It looks very beautiful There are many things in nature.

In many places natural chemical reactions take place. The water of the rivers look different due to these activities, which seems very attractive.

Hot springs burst in some countries. And the view they create from the distance with the steam also looks very beautiful & **the beauty of nature quotes**.

4. Nature has its own beauty with drawbacks

- When a tsunami hits the oceans, many people die while living on the beach.
- Heavy rains cause floods in low-lying areas. Cloudbursts greatly affect animal and human life.
- Forest fires kill many animals.

- Sometimes mountains suddenly fall in mountainous areas.
- Deforestation is on the rise due to which natural rainfall is declining and land erosion has increased.
- Man is progressing so much that he is slowly destroying **the beauty of nature**.
- Global warming has increased with the increase in pollution on earth.
- Man is ignoring the nature's law, due to which one or the other epidemic spreads and there is loss of life.
- Man is destroying the forests and we are suffering the consequences.
- Many countries have laws save the environment and the beauty of nature.
-

In order to maintain **the beauty of nature** and the law of nature, we have to take care of many things. Every problem has to be solved which poses a threat to our environment, atmosphere, living beings.

- Garbage should not be dumped in public places, seas, rivers, forests, etc.
- Animals should not be hunted.
- Control the pollution spread by human beings.
- Ban chemicals that pose a threat to our planet, humans, and other living things.
- Dams on rivers should be constructed in such a way that nature is not harmed.
- Recycle plastic and other waste items.
- Deforestation should be stopped completely and every effort should be made to save the wild animals.

- The ones that spread pollution should be replaced by electric vehicles or more bicycles.
- Use mostly public vehicles.
- One goal is to make it mandatory to plant at least 100
- trees every month.

9 798886 067736

Printed by Libri Plureos GmbH in Hamburg, Germany